SUBJECT MATTERS

John Grey

ISBN: 978-93-6354-435-2

First Edition: 2024
Rs. 200/-

Cyberwit.net
HIG 45 Kaushambi Kunj, Kalindipuram
Allahabad - 211011 (U.P.) India
http://www.cyberwit.net
Tel: +(91) 9415091004
E-mail: info@cyberwit.net

Printed at Repro India Limited.

Contents

Subject Matter

I need to stop writing poetry
about the smoky, red-veined wings
of the northeastern sawfly.
And, likewise, the Compton tortoiseshell
that flutters through the broadleaf woods.
The landscape doesn't need my advice.
Its creatures are what they are
without my slavish burnishing.

And no more poems of the city.
As if this cesspool on a grid
could ever care what stories people tell of it.
It's too big, too dirty, too noisy,
too bedeviling, for art.

And poems of other people
are sacrilege.
Words have no way of knowing
what's in their heads.
And when it comes to beauty,
the real thing is what you want.
Syllables, punctuation,
merely spoil the view.

And, most of all,
it's time to ditch
the mini-autobiographies.
Nothing imitates me as badly
as metaphors and pentameter.

My sicknesses
would be better served by a doctor
than publication.
As for my affairs of the heart -
see "sicknesses" above.

From now on
my poems will be
about nothing at all.
Yes I will miss subject matter.
But I must make sacrifices
if I'm to get nothing right.

At Sixteen, My Neighborhood

All morning, the woman
moves about the house,
still in her bathrobe.
Her husband left at sunrise

for his job in the foundry.
I sit on my stoop across the street.
She comes to the window
from time to time,

looks out for the mailman
for some reason I don't understand.
I'm indifferent to letters.
She seems to live for them.

Maybe a secret lover writes.
She still has most of her looks
and there's a shape inside
there somewhere.

It can't be from family.
Nobody's that anxious
to share in old grudges.
And she's certainly not

holding out for more bills.
I figure that she's at that age
where she has everything
she ever wanted

and she just plain
misses wanting it.
She waves to me
like she's admitting

to this clandestine affair
with her mysterious correspondent.
I wave back.
See, I knew I was right.

Steel Town

Clouds with a backwash of gray,
assault by chimney,

carbon residue clinging to the white,
factory churning out steel and landscape,

smog for hills, ash for trees,
air so pewter, lungs clang;

and then the slag heaps,
a perverse architect's model

of what a town should be;
look around, eyes burn,

breathe and
throat hacks like jays talk -

if you can't be bothered,
live there.

Shotgun

The wedding photo reeks of shotgun.
The bride is blank-faced.
The groom is caught by the lens mid-tremble.
The presence of a barrel, just off camera, is palpable.

They're your great-grandparents you tell me.
She was the daughter of a hard-drinking,
lazy slob of a farmer and his timid wife.
When he stomped through the house,
the children would scatter like chickens.
And he was the son of the widow
who ran the general store in town.
His only talent was getting the local girls pregnant –
including the wife who gave birth just six months later.

The finger on the trigger must have worked.
At least they made it through the ceremony,
lived together fifteen years, had four more kids,
during which his mother died suddenly and he
took over the store, ran it into bankruptcy
and then, at a time when he couldn't have been
more down on himself, took a shotgun –
maybe the shotgun that was almost
in the wedding picture, and was handed down
to the couple when her old man passed –
anyhow he somehow managed to place
the barrel against his temple, slip on
the kitchen's floors linoleum the moment
he pulled the trigger and blew a hole in the wall.

She had him put away then took the kids
and moved in with her older sister.
She didn't remarry.
But she held onto that wedding photo
which is why you're on the couch
this very instant, thumbing through an
old album and stopping at this very picture.
I sit beside you, as bored as a rainy-day child,
as I numbly watch you turn the pages
far too slowly for my lik8ng.

But there's a voice in my head that says,
"You stay boy or else."
It's followed by the cocking of a hammer.
Your Diner Awaits

Neon sign pulsing like a vein,
a beacon for the hungry – "Diner" –
okay, so maybe the "r" needs a little nudge
every now and then –
but trucks pull into the parking lot,
a car circles them with care.

Nothing much else happening at two a.m.,
just the deranged stumbling from the bars,
shaking like hanging lanterns
before stumbling into the gutter.
So cheap food, muddy coffee, surly waitress,
grim-faced cook, it is.
Plus six booths,
a counter crammed with bodies,
some stools that spin and some that don't,
conversation that occasionally touches a wound
but mostly rambles on, guttural and weary.

The bearded bald guy's been driving for someone
named Hopkins for going on thirty years.
The tattooed Slav only ever sees his wife on weekends.
The cook has a prison record.
He's reformed enough to hold down a lousy job.
And that waitress makes in tips
what she loses in flesh under the eyes.

Diner's not a cross-section of anything.
It's just people who are off to the side.
All complaints are the one complaint.
Every night is one just like it.

Life On Average

I wouldn't say this was a blue day.
Or an orange day.
Or black.
It's just average.
The conversation turns to
diapers and dog food.
The captivating face is leaden
with the hours of duty
stretched out ahead,
as far as the eyes can see,
which is, in this instance,
the kitchen ceiling
with its circling spider
and insidious damp spot.
It's not a day of bodies either
or the praiseworthy things
that blue jeans do for them.
It's not a hair day.
It's not a day of almandine skin.
bright green eyes,
or curious, winning wrist scents.
I'm raking leaves.
You're scrubbing window panes.
It's a day that has to be lived.
Otherwise, we'd never get to the next one.

Crossing America By Train

Corn grows up to the sky's rafters.
Wheat sprouts in rows a marathon long.
I'm crossing the great plains by train.
Boredom's tinged with gold
and very necessary.
After all, this is what we eat.
It has to grow somewhere
and there are so many of us
in this world to feed.

Tomorrow, we cross a mountain state
And the scenery will octuple down on splendor.
The viewing car will be a mob scene.
All eyes will be looking up.
Nothing jumpstarts awe
like snowy peaks in summer.

So I head for the dining car.
Here, in the flatlands,
I am assured I won't go hungry.
Mountain ranges stoke imagination
but are barren as the dead.

Jammed

At rush hour, we are all belligerent punks,
jammed from four lanes into two
just before a 95 overpass.
I'm behind a truck overflowing with scrap metal,
its tarp barely tied and flapping like an enemy flag.
On my left, a Chevy is trying to squeeze by
both of us in the breakdown lane.
Guy behind me is honking.
He wants me and my late Japanese model
to nudge forward an inch.
Under my breath, I'm like that homeless man
I saw berating the homeless woman –
all the cuss words I never use
come spilling out.
The guy in the Chevy is stuck,
can't get by the truck.
A Volkswagen that followed him
into the narrow no man's land
is now flashing his indicator
like he wants to ooze in front of me
if the scrap metal truck ever moves.
Fat chance, German beetle.
I'm in full military mode now.
Every inch of blacktop can only be won
by sacrifice of blood and sweat
and yes, vocabulary.
Somewhere behind me,
there's been a vainglorious cut-off attempt.
One guy is out of his car

and threatening another.
The villain of the piece doesn't flinch.
Nor is he about to roll down his window.
I feel that same rush of blood.
I'm itching to take somebody down
just for having nerve to be upon
this particular stretch of road
at this very moment.
Of course, when not at the wheel I'm not like this.
Remember my patience, my faith,
when everything was falling down around us.
I didn't give our debts the finger.
I didn't swerve in front of your mother
and send her flying into the median.
Everything that deserved
three blasts of my horn
got away without a sound.
Even those rear-enders I took in stride.
But meanwhile, back on the highway,
some guy on a motorcycle
is weaving in and out
of all these stationary vehicles
like he's fresh out of smart-aleck central.
The devil on my left shoulder
would love nothing more .than for me.
to suddenly pull out and send him flying
over the guard rail.
And yet, you and I live
between our own guard rails.
Anything that veers too close,
I rein back in...

That Old Eye For An Eye

I can't sleep, am drenched in the sweat of a man's last hours.
I'm alone, despite my wife beside me.
My mind is hangman and social worker, priest and warrior.
I press my head into the pillow. My thoughts know where I am.
They want me behind the glass panel with all the other fidgety witnesses.
Do I want to see the bastard fried - or would I rather lead the killer
away from the chair with a kindly hand,
sit him down for wine and understanding?
The folks outside the jail have dissipated, along with their placards.
The warden's home in bed. So is the one who pulled the switch.
How do their conflicted thoughts work for them, I wonder.
The execution went as planned.
Hey if someone killed the devil than that's okay with me.
Struggling to forgive the asshole 1 was merely assuaging my soul.
I mean nothing by it.
I'm with the vigilantes. No, wait a minute,
I don't believe in an eye for an eye.
It is midnight, a day beyond that long awaited execution
in a faraway Texas prison.
Killer in the chair - not exactly a magnet for sympathy.
And I'm in a deal with those bolts of juice.
But shouldn't I learn to be kind to the undeserving.
Then the hour repeats an old argument -
kill the beast and the dead go free.
But deep in my head,

the juiced guy screams for the rest of us.
The morning newspapers said that
a Mrs. Henry now feels something called closure.
That's also like execution. Only you get to live.

To The Poet On The Stage

Sorry but there's only
so much bitterness and heartbreak
a man can take.
Especially when it's not mine.

There's nothing wrong with wailing and moaning.
It's this tagging it as "art" that I have a problem with.
I get it. You're in pain.
But so are half the people on the planet.
And very few of them
ever get to bare their scars in public.

But here you are again,
up there on the podium,
in no doubt that others are keen to hear
from your pathetic life,
tearful inner child,
abomination of a family,
excruciating love affairs.

Whatever happened to
laugh and the worlds laughs with you?
To you, it's now
cry and you attract a crowd.
Yes, your misery gets attention.
For the rest of us poor souls,
there's nothing for it
but to weep into our own beer.
And they only serve coffee and soda here.

Then you have the nerve to say
that reading your poetry to others is therapy.
That would make your audience
the only psychoanalysts in town who pay their clients.

I admit that I've written to clear my head from time to time.
And I've felt the need to get the last hurt down on paper.
In times of old, they called that "hate mail."
Unlike you, I don't foist my miserable rage on anyone.
Not unless the trash barrel is a someone.

My problem is I came here for a good time.
Not that I'm complaining mind.
If I did, I'd be you.
From The Corpse To The Young Boy At The Wake

You're not dead.
So stand up.
Go to the window.
Look up at that
chancel of a sky.
The sun is at high noon.

Go outside.
Feel the warm in the air.
How it softly remonstrates
with the cool breeze.
And the grass of course,
soft enough for your toes
to eat.

I'm the one being
fitted for burial.

I'm no more, no less,
than the contents of a coffin.
I couldn't breathe
even if I had the recipe.
Like I said,
it's your noon.
Sample its pleasures.
It's hoary old midnight
for me.

And this is not a room
to be seen alive in.
It's merely an annex
to a graveyard.
Please don't despair.
And wipe that stupid sorrow
out of your eyes.

Go away from here.
Have a good time.
You don't have to justify
yourself with me.
And forget about paying your respects.
There's nobody at the register.

Suburban Dirt

Vince was only interested in a long-distance relationship.
Having Sarah so close by at all times was never going to work.
He kept getting feedback from her.
It wasn't always positive.
And she had no use for "The Lord Of The Rings."
That was the deal-breaker as far as he was concerned.
He ended it.
She went to an Ani DiFranco concert
to drown her sorrows in sorrows.
Vince passed his time in solitude
with generous helpings of self-abuse.
Vince's brother, Lee reckoned he was crazy
to break up with Sarah.
If he weren't so busy with his World of Warcraft,
he'd hit on her himself.
Vince's father, Luke has a secure job in a downtown insurance company.
He's the only one in the office who can change the printer's toner.
His wife, Janice, is a staunch advocate for the death penalty.
Sarah's old man, Rick has been called "dork" by more people than any other individual, living or dead.
His wife, Hannah chokes up when a celebrity dies.
Even if they're no longer a celebrity,
she still chokes up.
The last movie Jake saw in a cinema starred Billy Bob Thornton.
Jake's father Tom is in a nursing home.
He waxes nostalgically of a college panty-raid.
Sarah would sometimes prefer to be left alone.

Luke's name was once in a police blotter.
His brother Bob ran a red light but he was carrying Luke's ID.
Someone once told Lee he looks just like William Katt.
Lee still has no idea who William Katt is.
Back in the 80's, Janice came third in a chili cook-off.
But you would never know that from looking at her.
Hannah still doesn't trust ATMs.
Vince was embarrassed when some friends
spied him coming out of a Maroon 5 concert.
Sarah's spam filter accidentally deleted an email from an old friend.
She spends her nights exploring on-line dating tips.
Rick once had a chance to go in with a buddy on a Popeye's franchise.
Sadly, he couldn't come up with the ready.
Janice is upset because she has nothing worth selling on Ebay.
Hannah's dream is to enter into rehab.
But she has to get herself hooked on something first.

Time To Leave

In the magic air, the hushed autumn whispers,
leaves skim lawns, static-y shadows
pace the edges, birds winged-up,
prepare for the trip south.

We stroll these halls of ancient torture,
gold and red, the sky's palette,
you like Pinturicchio's "Portrait Of A Boy"
with your young face, long flap of hair,
and the beginnings of a beard aging your soft chin,
and me beside you, anxious to be moving on,
as old school buildings pretend to be real substance,
even as wings beat in the trees above.

These feathered visitors have done as much as they can
in the summer months just as we are finished
with the preparation, can only cast off from here,
even if we lack the flying apparatus.

But my imagination's like nothing I have
known up to now, and the coming twilight
mirrors the dream world you plan to enter into –
one day, we said – and repeated like a child's
alphabet – and now one day is here.
Unlike the birds, every direction is south to us.

Beth And The Coffee Cup

Your hand can really wrap around a cup and tighten.
Be thankful it's not your throat.
Long after you've drunk its contents,
you feel for insight in its smooth china surface,
beyond its current shape back to manufacture,
prototype, planning, even its ingredients
deep in the earth.
When the skin below your eye is bruised,
you're out to feel the hurt in everything.
How willing is the coffee cup to be here,
its steaming liquid to be drunk,
its small bowed handle to be threaded
by a shaking finger.
"Want another?" I ask, knowing you'd
rather sip than talk just now.
And you've no wish to ask,
"Why do I have such lousy luck with men?"
More coffee steams between the lips
so they won't say these words.
And you grip the cup more like a vise than ever.
Hold hard enough, you hold together.
What doesn't drop can't shatter.

Night Nurse Blues

All patients start out
in the same immaculate bed -

but some leave in a glow,
others in a box -

yet, healing and dying,
are both draped in white
and smell of such cleanliness -

so why do they go their separate ways?

late at night,
I bring to each, in turn,
pills on a tray,
water in a tumbler
to wash them down -

I do some people more than good
and others, nothing at all -

this job had no idea
if it's a ladder
or a mineshaft.

A Time When I Press Like

In tree shadow,
Jeremiah sprawls,
hands under head,
cap over eyes,
snores loud and heart-shaped.

At stream's edge,
Casey, barefoot,
washes, cleans,
body and clothes,
soft brown skin,
many-hued dresses,
as her humming
rides the slow but ceaseless current
in the warm of the afternoon.

Geese skim back and forth
across the water.
Andrew in a small canoe
threads them as he paddles upstream.
Back against oak tree,
June perches a book on her chin,
dozes into another story.

Children toss Frisbees,
pick mulberries,
sweat enough purple

to sustain their giggles
until nightfall.

A wisp of breeze
has chosen this spot to blow.

Your Book

Perusing this book
is as hard on the eyes
as digging into hard ground
is on the hands and shoulders.

The print is old, decaying.
The leaves have the consistency of shrouds.
And the cover surely was someone's skin,
back before the flailing.

There are so many words you've never heard spoken.
So many dark secrets – vile
yet a siren song to your curiosity.

"Read no further" one page cautions.
"You have been warned" says another.

But trembling, fearful, yet as inquisitive as a child,
you venture on, deeper into chapters
more repellant by the paragraph,
but equally fascinating,
to a point where the book feels like part of you,
and there is no stopping,
no letting go.

It's no longer the eyes that ache.
Your hands, your shoulders, throb
as if you really have been digging.

And into hard ground
that still cracks open
from the sheer relentlessness
of your mind's shovel.

Then you come to the end,
weakened but still defiant.
You close the cover
and your body reluctantly shuts down.

Perusing the book
is like opening a grave at midnight.
With a sigh of relief,
you discover the body is your own.

Danielle

Danielle, I left you
behind in Santa Fe
so I could learn
more about you.

Providence has become a combination
of your personal history
and a psychologist's insights.
Everywhere I go

I see places you've never been.
Every new feeling
is one I never had toward you.
And I don't answer your emails,

don't even read them in fact,
because they would just fog up
this amazing clarity
my head has taken on

since I returned to my old hangouts.
And please stop calling.
The sound of your voice
is not helping your cause any.

Only silence can do that.
Your total absence
really is a great teacher.
Did you know that

Danielle 101 is a walk
along the riverbank,
taking in the sights, the sounds,
that are there for my enjoyment,

not my indictment.
It has occurred to me
that we never were
meant for each other.

Providence is more than a city.
It's a conclusion.
I'm living on my own.
It's like I'm really with someone at last.
From The Gut

The poet was reading, in a bar,
his latest great work,
page after page of scarifying,
self-immolating, soul-flagellating, verse.
A dozen people were listening to him.
But two men, both drunk,
were being loud and obnoxious.
The poet asked them to quiet down
as people wanted to hear.
One of the men flew into a rage.
The other tried to hold him back,
but to no avail.
The big galoot grabbed the poem
out of the poet's hand
and tore it to shreds.
Then he grabbed the poor guy
by the throat

and slammed him against the wall.
The audience was stunned at first
as the poet, when he could
momentarily free his throat
from his assailant's raw grip,
shouted something about
"evolution" and "Neanderthal."
His twelve fans packed up their stuff
and left.
They were willing to listen
to other's troubles
but didn't want to redden the bar floor
with any of their own.
The bartender came over
and tried to put a stop to the one-sided fight.
With the help of the man's buddy,
he was finally able to separate the two.
The poet lay bleeding.
The honor of the other was brutally satisfied.
"Are you okay?" asked the bar-tender of
the broken scrunched up figure of the versifier.
A simple "yes" or "no" was out of the question.

Life With The Sounds

When it came to the arguments,
I had an obstructed view,
namely the wall that separated
their apartment from mine.
But the audio was loud and clear
even if I didn't want to hear.

There was no need to cock my ear
for her sobbing,
or his stumbling through the door
late on a payday evening.
Even if the couple didn't live with me.
their relationship did.

The night she overdosed,
the whine of an ambulance
occupied my kitchen.
Heavy footsteps down the hall
spent time in my parlor,
as did his voice crying out.
"Will she be okay."

When she was released from hospital
a day later,
they were so quiet
that they moved completely out of my place.
But they were back a month later
with more fights, more drinking, more tears.

I abandoned those digs for a complex
where my next door neighbor
was a ballerina
who played her music in my shower stall
and whose toes.
soft but squeaky,
shared living space with my own bare feet.
As a roommate, the sounds she made were perfect.
Rent was cheap, utilities included:
gas, electricity and pas de deux.

Roommate

My roommate, death,
is busy typing up a letter –
    what's your social security number,
    he asks –
I hated him at first
but now,
in my weakened state,
I've grown attached
to his solemn presence –
    sometimes
    I fake a heart attack
    just to mess up his timeline –
or I say,
"I'm feeling much better"
even when I'm not –
    he's not easily cheated
    but I'm his equal in dark humor –
besides, the number I gave him
    is yours.

An Abandoned Country Graveyard

Some crosses and stones survive,
but, sadly, most of the graves are overgrown,
yet weeds and wildflowers don't know from sacrilege,
have their own ways of living and dying.

But there are names and dates
still visible to the eyes and fingers,
and lives lived, from two months to eighty-five years,
and near to the place where they happened.

From the darkness which is death,
I rescue an image of somebody named Nathaniel,
a woman, Elizabeth, a child Rachel,
and a Samuel, a Ruth, and a Winthrop.

Many tracks, silent spoors, cloaked footprints,
but all to a purpose of their own.
Before these pioneers were forgotten,
something brought them where they are.

In Northern New Hampshire

An abandoned farmland,
set free from machinery,
goes wild

while the tractor rusts
like old train lines

and the farmhouse
is no more than a basement

and a framed
"Bless Our Home"
behind broken glass

as trees slowly encroach,
put things back
the way they were
before settlement

now that fact
has overwhelmed faith

and the human graves
must compete
with the living moles
and groundhogs

and the breeze whispers
just enough to be imagined -

whoever you were,
you have been replaced.

Frog Tales

So many frogs leaping across
the field after rain,
trying to catch one
is like trying to catch the lot.
All green, all leaping,
no uniqueness,
merely tiny hopping pieces
of the master frog,
spreading out to all corners
of the soggy earth.

I kept a frog once, scooped it
out of a pond, stored it in a bottle
with nail-pricked lid to give it air.
Didn't know then that it needed more
than odd moments with my curious face
through glass to sustain it.
Didn't appreciate that whatever is separated
from the tribe of itself
cannot be enough of a thing to survive.
It struggled to be whole,
to be inclusive.
It died eventually,
hard up against the wall we shared.

This Odd Sister

Yes, she's a little mad
but only to the discerning observer.
And she doesn't go completely off the rails
but takes a small step
to the right here, the left here,
just so she can stay a little disconnected,
Everyone else has their sense
and clings to it fiercely.
She lets slightly loose from time to time
just so sanity won't get too full of itself.
She's always willing to agree
with what you say
but with her fingers crossed
behind her back.
And she spits when required
and scratches where it itches.
She likes to think that makes her dangerous.

Hit On At The Pool

You can't be alone, not with a beast of conceit
towering over you. Yet you rub mulberry into
your hands and lips, suddenly bloom,
ripe for embrace, breathless and brown-haired –
your own style and not be imprisoned by his.
Now, he's just another guy with sweaty needs,
once lost for good in his own self-love,
now hammering on your sea-gull smile – let me in –
I'm handsome – I'm double jointed – let me in.

But you're strong enough so he doesn't rub
off on you. He's half a poolside romance but
your heart won't complete the math for him.
He may as well flop back in the water, be just
another ripple. Or stroke his own beleaguered hair.
Flex his muscles until his upper arms vibrate.
There's an odd reality to no longer being
the gawky girl. The heroes turn villains. And
from there, the only work available is as an extra.

You're young yet. There'll be time enough
for tenderness. Even young pigeons try out
their wings before they bother procreating.
To him, you're Miss Dashed Hopes of 2023.
But you don't gloat on it. Not while his bad temper
saps his energy. Not while he shrinks down to
some overage spoiled child. Not while his
eyes turn away and his fingers play with pebbles.
Then he departs, leaves you with the solitude you sought.
Your self-esteem has clearly been worth it.

The Prowling Fox

The fox watches
through dark leaves,
is a shadow
stalking shadows.

The sun's goodbye
turns the forest's wheel,
releases small
packed-in mammals.

The fox
listens for the merest footfall,
sniffs out the abiding scents.

It moves slowly,
ever slowly,
on the way
to a rapid kill.

\

The Fruit

The fruit is all good.
She imagines herself in the garden of Eden.
So what if it's just a kitchen.
This one is rightfully hard.
This one is tender and soft.
Unzip the rind
and she delights in the pale flesh.
Then she tilts her head back
to drink down the passion fruit juice.
It amazes her what she can get her hands around,
how her taste buds respond,
what a trip to the market
can bring into her world.
The bite has replaced romance
and she can't say that she misses the latter.
Not while she can nibble.
Not while the blemished and the shiny
both have such appeal.
From the apples to the oranges,
it's all hers and hers alone.
Feeling old, fermented and fetid herself these days,
she can still appreciate a ripeness.

For Rene To Meet A Guy Worth Her Life-time

All it would take
is a large rotating fiery cloud
of interstellar dust and gas
accelerated by shockwave,
then contracting,
from more shock,
this time a nearby supernova,
into a ball of fire

while larger fragments of hot debris
clump together into planets,
spend five and a half billion years cooling,
and, on one of these new worlds,
chemical reactions spawn nucleobases,
amino acids,
primitive forms of life
that slowly,
over many more millions of years,
evolve into three or four
decent, hard-working,
marriageable young guys
standing at the bar,
sipping martinis
that they almost spill
when you enter.

This is where patience comes in.

In Search Of Yesterday In New Hampshire

Stone walls mark the edges
of overgrown pastures.

So many remnants
of a civilization lost to all
but some memories.

Houses have been demolished,
or burnt, or overgrown,
but cellar holes hold out,
with their jigsaw fieldstones
and hardy blocks of granite.

I come across a rusty tractor
and a cameo wedged in dirt.
And is that a comb?
And, over there, a kettle?

Strangest of all
is an oak tree
that's grown up around
a stretch of barbed wire,
that's cut into its trunk
for a hundred years.

Such an awkward coming together
of man and nature.
Most aren't as obvious
but there are many more like this.

From Out Of The Mouth Of The Useless

Oh great plumber woman,
shelter me with your wiry arms,
skillful hands,
for I have a leaking pipe
that needs patching,
a faucet too tough to turn,
a shower flow
sputtering and cold.

And you,
my beloved electrician goddess,
kiss me while you mend those wires,
and I'll be assured
that any buzz I feel
will be from passion
and not high voltage.

Carpenter angel,
wonderous tailor beauty,
exquisite mechanic-ess,
you are the lovers I seek
in this modern world.
where looking after myself
is no longer a one-man job.

I am desirous of the useful,
enamored of the trade.
And you are needed now.
I assure you, I can pay…
with the rest of my life
if I have to.

The Flautist On The Romanian Hillside

In the name of all remoteness, what have we here.
A shepherd boy is playing on a flute.
He doesn't mind the chill and his sheep pay heed.
And, I'm sure, somewhere beyond the forest wall,
the wolves draw close, listen in.

In the shadow of the rearguard mountains,
where the blue lake improvises on a fading sun,
music circles the flock like a lariat of sound,
wraps around each unuttered bleat,
lifts the fluttering earlobes skyward.

Who else can be so young with hair so black and matted,
and clothes so thin, the wind holds off in sympathy.
But notes don't know where the lips come from.
Cocooned in air, they're out like butterflies.

What happened to the wild? Sound has conquered.
Tunes have answered deepest fears.
Beasts no longer tremble. Man becomes less a conscious thing.
Even on death, is written a staff, a scale or two
The reeds are heaven, the face is stony uplands.

The Realtor

To her,
the town was no more
than an advertising circular

with every house
on every street listed,
each with a price
to buy, to sell,

but only through her
and not
her competitor realtors.

As for the people,
they were figures,
calculations, estimates,
owners and buyers,
downsizers and new families
needing some place roomier.

To her,
the town
was an entity
that bought and sold itself
on a regular basis.

From time to time,
she peeked in the mirror,
so she wouldn't forget
what a commission looked like.

A Memory In Black And White

She associates black and white
with the dead.
All of the actors on Turner Classic Movies
are gone.
So are the solemn faces
in the train on the way to the death camp.

The films remind her of her childhood,
when she sat in the dark,
amazed at the sights on the screen.
And as for that locomotive
about to leave the station –
women in plain dresses, babushkas,
men in the coats
they will soon enough shrink into,
SS smiling for the camera –
the end of her childhood
came with its own funeral.

Her grandchildren
cannot bear to watch
those flickering black and white images.
To them, if it's not in color,
then it isn't real.
She says in reply,
the glamorous don't need color,
the evil don't deserve it.

Naming The Streets

I have a strange relationship with streets,
how Prairie grows tenements
in lieu of stalks of golden wheat
and Westminster is about as parliamentary
as a blurred shout from a passing car.
I enjoy the paradox, the irony,
as I walk these well-marked lies,
relish the fact that a long time ago,
when these things were named, someone
did their bit for the modest end of history
and got it totally wrong.
The locals laugh at me.
My curiosity is out of place.
Where are the prairies, where are
the Westminsters, in these narrow
Providence backlots?
What inspired the names?
It couldn't have been these roadways.
Even then, they must have been
nothing more than mudheaps,
dug up by bullock dray and horse hoof,
the bullying trudge of early migrants
on the way home from factory work.
I imagine a bespectacled clerk from some
obscure city agency, face as narrow as a bean,
scratching the numbness from his chin,
lost in a world of responsibility and chaos,
in his early twenties, new to the east,
born in Nebraska, where skies are everywhere

and don't just circle and swoop
between the high rises.
These inner suburbab streets,
huddled like cold fingers at
the Main Street's fire,
would have thwarted him then as they do me now.
What would I have called them?
These grids suggest nothing,
are as unforthcoming
as government workers.
He must have shrugged his shoulders,
bones rising like wings
of birds familiar to his youth,
head dropping out of
this neck bone of pressure
onto the lap of his past.
After all, when there's no other option,
it's the remembering that reminds you.
The farmhouses, red as carnelian,
rising out of the powdery midwestern sun.
The pictures of a tourist's London
falling out of a grandfather's album
like tears.
Forget the urban squabble,
the pitiless demands of the new.
It's those roads back to what you were
that connect you to here,
that you'd give names
like Prairie or Westminster.
Perfect names.
Even if the streets are less so.

My Home Alone Story

There was that hour
when I was in the house alone,
outside was on the cusp of light and dark,
and I was on a similar verge,
old enough to be on my own,
but still a baby when it came
to creaking floors, rustling curtains,
and the very thought of basements.

That terrified courage
could only be relieved
by a car in the driveway,
garage door grinding open,
key in the lock,
the sound of my name
spoken by a familiar other.

Television couldn't protect me.
Nor the schoolbooks I opened,
as I sat on the floor,
puzzled over homework.
Not when shadows lengthened by the moment.
Mice ran relays inside the walls.
And thunderstorms hung around the horizon
like punks under a street lamp.

But when my mother came home,
there were no more dangers.
Just bills on the table.
And her turn to be afraid.

Tugboat

It's like a variation on a lightbulb joke.
How many tugboats does it take to fill a giant tanker?
The real answer is something like,
more than the total of every tugboat on duty
in every port on the entire Eastern seaboard.
But there's a second question that comes to mind.
How many tugboats does it take to lead
one of those ocean-going behemoths into the dock?
The answer, this time, is twenty six feet long,
with a thousand horsepower diesel engine
and enough nautical muscle memory
to nudge three football fields of ship into its harbor berth.

The tugboat captain would be bamboozled
if he ever stepped onto a tanker's bridge.
His vessel keeps things simple.
Even his own computer he's reluctant to have on board.
To him, the old tug is no different from his first fishing boat.
Even in the densest of harbors, he could have steered it blindfold.
His boat extends his body to the water and below.
It feels its way. And he feels the feelings.

Later, on the dock, he puffs on a cigarette,
looks up at the Goliath that he squeezed into a David.
His smile is wider than Goliath's stern to bow.

The Tale The Dead Tell

I drive by the crime scene,
an unprepossessing two story Cape,
its driveway, its stoop,
bordered off with yellow tape.

And I hike through the woods
to what remains of the abandoned farmhouse,
windows shattered, bindweed sprouting
through cracks in the parlor,
front door half-hanging from rusty hinges,
barn-swallow nests in roof timbers,
forest creeping in from all sides.

Many people gather at the crime scene.
There's a television camera
and some guy in a suit
poking his microphone
in the face of the neighbors.

It's just me by the fallen fence,
the rain-soaked mattress,
the rabbits digging
in what used to be a garden.

Murdered in cold blood,
murdered by tough truths,
all these faces or just the one,
cops or white-tailed deer,
bloodstains or tattered curtains,
loud muttering or quiet poetry.

Feminine

It's always a woman's fault.
Eve's temptation, Pandora opening her box,
Kali, Ereshkigal and Morrigan...
not a male hormone among them.
So tell me, Gale, what's the plan?
Will I die of something you do?

But then I think of the Earth Mother,
my own mother,
giving birth, bestowing life
on creatures like me.
Throw in Ishtar, Isis, Cybele...
without all this feminine fertility
I wouldn't be around
to complain about what's killing me.

It's not a plan,
it's a dichotomy.
Life's a gift.
The giver wants it back.

Sisters

You can have one. You can have more than one.
It was never my choice though. I came later.
Anyway, I would have asked for a bike.
Or a cricket bat. Or a dozen comic books, Superman preferred.

They can act like second mothers. They do.
Or like more of a brat than I was. Occasionally.
I could have done with a brother, now that I think about it.
Someone to look up to. All I had was the ceiling.

They can work for a short time doing mundane tasks. Mine did.
Then get married. Mine did that also.
The most precious gift to me was their leaving.
Just at the age when I needed a room of my own, I had one.

And they can have kids. They can have more than one.
They can annoy their uncle or make him want one of his own.
They did both. Some offspring were brothers. Some were sisters too.
But they all retreated to their own homes when it was time.

They can die young. They can live on despite cancer and Parkinson's.
Mine did. Mine have. I have been dutiful in sympathizing. Even from afar.
They can make you wonder if we ever were a family. Or just the opposite.
Get you feeling like we're all forty years younger. They do both.

You can think of them. They can be totally absent from your thoughts
for a week or more. My mind goes through phases. My heart, also.
They can live their own lives. They can affect the lives of others.
I've felt the separation. I've experienced the pull.

You can have three. You can have none.
Looking back, I accept that having three was for the best.
They're a part of who I am. My aim therefore
is to restore them to their prominence.

Dump Stories

Stay away from the dump, our mother said.
It was full of rats, fleas, diseases.
We wondered why there were such places
where you could die just by being there.

And yet, like clockwork, the green
trash bags collected on the sidewalk
every Tuesday evening. We knew where
they were headed. The evil...we were part of it.

Meanwhile, we crossed the roadway
where the kid was hit.
Hot summer days, we swam in the lake
where three drowned.

Never heard of anyone dying in the dump
though we could see its hills of trash
from the highway, see people with their
refrigerators, TV's, trucks, large and small,

a community of fellow travelers
in sickness... as we passed crosses,
flowers, in memory of car crash victims.
And what about the news in the paper...

woman beaten to death by husband,
old man slips on soap, smacks his
head against the bath-tub, someone
electrocuted in his basement,

home heater explodes, three
children burnt to death.
It seemed like the place most warned against
was the safest to be.

And yet, for all the evidence, we never
did play in the dump's benevolent junk piles,
anodyne old cars, harmless critters.
We stayed secure in the real danger.

The Life They Leave Me With

Sun setting, wind picking up, I stalk the lowly Providence River
on its last throes before it enters Narragansett Bay.
Thousands of miles away, the last of my sisters has died.
The family I was born into is no more.

I am not under any pledge of silence but I am avoiding people
just in case they want a word from me.
And I shut out the noise of this city for memory of another.
My mother has my hand this time and the day is warm and clear

as we stroll down Queen Street, stop for every shop window.
The old picture palaces beckon with their movie posters
and gilded, grand foyers. But then I follow her
into this cavernous department store, a glittering melee

of ten thousand lives' worth of possessions. We buy nothing.
It is enough to just look. My imagination begins here.
Then I'm with my oldest sister. We are in a book store.
My prize for being with her is an adventure story,

with a front cover of a Spitfire pilot in bomber jacket
engaged in aerial combat with a Messerschmitt.
And that's me with my middle sister. She lifts me
up onto a stool at the Malt Shop counter.

On a hot summer's day, my face wears what drops
of a milk shake my tongue cannot get to first.
Lastly, I'm with my youngest sister, who's older
than I am by six years. We're at the local cheap movie house.

She plunks me down the front, retreats to the back seats
with her girlfriends and some boys. The screen takes
up all of my eyes and then some. But, when the show ends
and I go to find her, many years pass. I receive a phone call

in the early hours. She has passed away. I am all that's left.
And nothing says that better than this stroll beside the Providence river.
The sun dips below the hurricane barrier, orange flame
fuses with red, sends sparks into the cloudless darkening sky.

Our Old House

Our old house is now a fever in the brain.
It's buttons loose that no one cares to mend.
It's creaking bones. It's chill getting in
through gaps in the windows.
You don't understand.
There are people locked up in there,
They no longer recognize me.
They live in fog and thickening of the arteries.
One day, they will set fire to themselves.
But, for now, they pretend the matches are children.

I am weary from thinking about our old house.
A ghost peaks out of the window.
Another bends over the stove.
Can you believe it but one of these phantoms
is even singing in a harsh, decrepit voice.
It is a dirge not a song of joy.

Why won't someone turn on the lights in our old house.
The rats have left. Why not the white-haired captain.
The dribbling first mate.
But our old house is misapplied rouge, smudged lipstick,
hopeless and heartless and as dry as a sermon.
We move about but it never does.
We change our address but it stays put
with the earth that owns it.
Some days it wraps a shredded scarf around its rooftop.
Some nights, it cuts itself, bleeds the darkest blood.

Magician On The Stairs

Will he pull a rabbit from his hat today
or merely hover on the third step,
clutching the railing,
as sun through window spotlights
his pale, splotchy, wrinkled face?
Are card tricks on the cards?
Or can he saw a woman in half
and which woman?
There's twelve stairs in all
and, for every one,
the shine has something different
for his eyes, his skin, his thin gray hair, to say.
So what about the magic wand?
And the flock of doves eagerly awaiting
takeoff from his sleeves?
The race between regrets and conjuring.
is a slow contest because it's morning
and the legs are still unsteady
even if the hands are quick.
And I'm an audience of one,
spending a weekend in his home away
from all our homes.
He's frail, more frail than the last time I was here.
Does that mean the rings aren't linked after all?
Or there's a hole in the table
where the ball drops through?
I greet him with an arm around his shoulder.
Will he say, "I love you" or "Pick a card, any card"?
Instead, he mutters, "Your mother is a good woman."
He's asking for forgiveness,
the ultimate misdirection.

Dive Position

I'm at the very tip of the board,
bent like a bow
with my arms stretched outward.
Below me are lab rats,
women in floral hats,
impressionist painters,
illusions of love,
gulls and picknickers,
climaxes and stood-up dates,
unreality and locality,
Bohemia, Dada,
an inexplicable light,
a bird on a bough,
Morris dancers, cancer cells,
funeral marches, shrouds,
the beautiful and the dumb.
I've suffered from expectations long enough.
It's time for a happy accident.

Sea-Side Town In November

You wouldn't believe
what your absence has done
to the days.
No need for me to rewrite
"The Sorrows Of Young Werther."
Three o'clock in the afternoon
does it for me.

I walk the streets,
shivering and alone.
There's one restaurant still open,
home to the locals
who gather and drink
and celebrate the exit
of the likes of me.
I can remember
the two of us discussing
what it must be like around here
in winter.
And I'm counting down Goethe
and Swinburne and Plath
and every other melancholy soul
until the day I find out.

Does the sea freeze? Do fish die of the cold?
Does snow blanket sand?
And what about the trees,
leaves wasted,
stripped down to the bones?
Sure I know it's November
but it never used to be.

Adrift

Barely moving, adrift,
sailboat in deep fog,
the extraordinary sailor
I imagined myself to be
is waiting for that mist to lift,
the wind to pick up,
for his surrounds to be more substantial,
more familiar,
and for the unseen gulls to stop laughing.

This is an awkward situation,
where most of what is real
is unavailable to me,
and my self-reliance frays
like the oldest rope in the rigging.

My confidence is a game
played with weather and forestay,
spreader and shroud.
Cocooned like this,
someone else is dealing,
rattling the silent dice.

I'm not dead
but my confidence is in mourning
That's why ghosts gather.
And I feel more like a weightless soul
than 170 pounds of body.

Or a shadow.
Or a dream.
But not a pilot.
Not enough to guide me home.
For this place is a secret.
I've a feeling it plans to keep it.

You Would Never Know I Was Here

For frenzy
there's the sea itself,
sawgrass whipped up
by the wind,
or two gulls
squabbling over a fish carcass.

And for relative calm,
the pines,
tall and restrained,
and the warblers among them,
songs drowned by crashing waves,
but heard within the colony.

Near stillness
is the tide pool,
an urchin
like half a ball
covered with spikes,
a fiddler crab
barely bigger than a thumbnail,
and tiny fish
darting in and out of rock cover.

Here is the end of my mission -
not the chopped-up angry waves,
not their fuzzing foam
as they slap against the shore,
not even the sunrays

that bear down on the bare skin
of the true believers.

Instead, I'm enrapt
in this most minute activity.
If it weren't for breath,
I wouldn't know I was here.

July In New England

Heat comes down
like it's raining air,
rises up like cow patty smell,
thoughts erupt,
children strike up arguments
like matches,
blood boils, bubbles,
wind whips whatever
skin its fancies,
welts of summer,
scars of hunger for the cool;

and whoever first
thought of windows
thick as spectacles for the blind
is pleading from
the heavy curtain shadows,
just as reality swears
off family,
especially the brawling kind,
and a woman dusts
my earlobes with her anger;

walls of my house melt,
ceiling liquefies,
roof is the wings of a dead crow,
can't fly,
craps in on itself,
temperature replaces gas bills

on my enemies' list,
the sordid details of humidity
are spelled out in greasy sweat
for all to see
and humiliate me;

the ones who died
years ago don't know
how lucky they are,
underground dwellers of the desert,
cool as rattle-snakes,
while the rest of us
beach ourselves on the
shores of beer,
wait for our lungs to collapse;

damn is the new capital of rooms,
hell is the mind on mercury,
a weather forecaster speaks
from the fringes of the doomed planet...
your children will strangle each other
before this is through;

if only it would rain,
a storm would do me like drugs,
I don't care about thunder,
it speaks my language,
and lightning works for me
as long as it strikes others...
thankfully the kids are punching each other.
now which of them is lightning?
now which is thunder?

It's All In The Webbing

The first web is light and thin,
a trailer for the giant silken main feature
farther down the path.
That first web is barely there,
like a child's breath on the skin,
whisked away with a swift backhand.

But then comes the web so huge
not even dew can drip its way around
the outer anchor lines.
The sun flatters,
dazzles these scattered jewels,
a brilliant light to celebrate
a spider's perfect handiwork.

It's either go around
or risk being the next beetle,
next moth, trapped in that arachnid's lair.
Or, at best, I'll be picking bits
of thread from my clothing
for a week while, all the time,
wondering if the creator of this handiwork
is crawling somewhere on my body.

The first web is a skirmish, I figure.
The second web is all out war.
Or the first web is a date.
The second web is marriage.

Or maybe they're both just webs,
one more complex than the other.
Or only the first is a web.
The second may well be two conjoined spiders.

Rabbit Hunters

Off they go into the woods
on a rabbit hunt.
There must be about ten of them in all,
dressed in orange, wielding rifles,
ready and willing to take potshots
at the Easter Bunny, Peter Cottontail,
or anything soft and furry
that dares hop into their sights.

Maybe two of them
are inspired by warm memories
of their mother's rabbit stew.
And there's another who can't abide
those Energizer Bunny ads.
And one poor soul whose mother
bored his childhood
by reading aloud from
"The Velveteen Rabbit."

There could even be a couple
of Elmer Fudd apologists.
He was their kind after all –
a hunter with a Bugs Bunny complex.
I can imagine a cry,
from deep in the forest,
after a successful kill.
"I'll give you What's Up Doc, you varmint!"

I can't write the rabbit's poem.
There's no way for me
into the head of that furry flash.
To be honest, I'm hardly more equipped
to slip inside a hunter's mind.
What gratification can there be
in coming out on top in a contest so one-sided?
A boxing ref would call it "no contest"
before the bell was rung.

I watch the hunters go in.
I seem them emerge later,
some clutching rabbit corpses, some not.
Their secret is safe from me.

Kid Ray

Kids are out playing street hockey.
Orange pucks are flying around.

One kid's bigger than the others,
Ray, I think his name is,
because all the kids on the sidelines
are shouting, "Shoot it Ray!"
or "Thump him Ray!"

But Ray neither shoots nor thumps.
One whack of his blade
against that flying puck
and he could drive it into somebody's face,
smash his nose.
An elbow into an opponent's midriff
and who knows how many ribs would bust.

So he makes gentle passes.
He holds up at the point of a collision.

Ray's grown so fast,
he refuses to occupy his body.

This River

Current is the main attraction here.
In a world of brief thirst quenching
and occasional rain, it celebrates
its own victory party over landscape,
distance, fish and people.
It's like thick papers on eternity,
always open at the same unfinishable page.
What do I have to measure against it?
A long ago childhood? A day that stretches
interminably in a year I can't believe is almost gone?
Dragonflies buzz about the river's surface,
briefer lives than mine though made bearable I'm sure
by the complete absence of philosophy.
They accept the moment though not the religion.
I look down for my reflection.
It breaks up before it forms.

A Kind Of Money

Company is a kind of money.
The more you accumulate,
the wealthier you feel.
But what about the times
when you empty out your pockets,
looking for change, a coin, anything
and there's nothing there
but shredded cloth.
I'm up in my room alone.
An entire monetary system goes
on without me.
The people on the street
have so much to spend on each other
but none left over for me.
The telephone doesn't ring.
No knock on the door.
The letters don't arrive.
And then there's love,
that ritual begging,
the heart upraised like a cup.
Please fill it, I ask,
with just enough so I can start
feeling good about myself again.
But no one's buying that line.
This one doesn't want to see me.
That one could care less.
Company is a kind of money and
I don't have a penny to my name.
Sure I need to earn some.
But no one that I've ever known
is hiring.

Vanishing Hitchhiker

There's still a highway
and more than enough land to traverse.
And cars of course.
Plus a whole lot of trucks.

But there is nobody at the side of the road
with their belongings on their back
and thumbs in the air.
So no one is stopping.

The journey is there
as it has always been
but, whatever it promises,
no one's taking the mileage up on it.

So, from town to town,
landscape to landscape,
there are no engrossing
conversations between strangers.
No life stories.
No ruminating on the freedom of the great outdoors.
No two voices singing along to songs on the radio.
No older driver who suddenly feels nostalgic
for the trip he never took
when he was young.

The highway still looks the part,
as does the country it crosses.

But the cars, the trucks,
they're just traffic these days.
And the people are strictly behind the wheel
or a familiar passenger.

There's no inclination to travel rough.
There are less thumbs than there used to be.

ACKNOWLEDGEMENTS

A Kind Of Money	Wise Owl
A Memory In Black And White	Old Red Kimono
A Time When I Press Like	Avant Appalachia
Adrift	
	Tenth Muse
An Abandoned Country Graveyard	Clamor
At Sixteen, My Neighborhood	Pulsar
Beth And The Coffee Cup	San Antonio Review
Crossing America By Train	Schuylkill Valley
	Review
Danielle	Steam Ticket
Dive Position	Lullwater Review
Dump Stories	Uppagas
Feminine	Amulet
For Rene To Meet A Guy Worth	Whistling Shade
	Her Lifetime
Frog Tales	NOD Magazine
From Out Of The Mouth Of	US1 Worksheets
	The Useless
From The Corpse To The Young	Umbrella Factory
	Boy At The Wake
From The Gut	Door Is A Jar
Hit On At The Pool	California Quarterly
In Northern New Hampshire	Pinyon Review
In Search Of Yesterday In New	Isotrope
	Hampshire
It's All In The Webbing	Kennings
Jammed	Bethlehem Writer's
	Roundtable

July In New England	Havik
Kid Ray	Illya's Honey
Life On Average	Schuylkill Valley Review
Life With The Sounds	Off Course
Magician On The Stairs	Firelight
My Home Alone Story	EKL Review
Naming The Streets	Pikeville Review
Night Nurse Blues	Abbey
Our Old House	South Florida Poetry Journal
Rabbit Hunters	Floyd County Moonshine
Roommate	Shot Glass Journal
Seaside Town In November	Tenth Muse
Shotgun	Floyd County Moonshine
Sisters	Suisin Valley Review
Steel Town	Poetry Superhighway
Subject Matter	Chronopolis
Suburban Dirt	Lost Pilots
That Old Eye For An Eye	Adelaide Literary Magazine
The Flautist On The Romanian	Fourth And Sycamore Hillside
The Fruit	Triggerfish
The Life They Leave Me With	Trajectory
The Prowling Fox	Blueline
The Realtor	Abbey
The Tale The Dead Tell	Trajectory
This Odd Sister	Trajectory
This River	Doubly Mad

Time To Leave	Cool Beans Lit
To The Poet On The Stage	In Between Hangovers
Tugboat	Perceptions
You Would Never Know I Was Here	Tenth Muse
Your Book	La Presa
Your Diner Awaits	Floyd County Moonshine

www.ingramcontent.com/pod-product-compliance
Lightning Source LLC
LaVergne TN
LVHW091124150826
845673LV00002B/959

* 9 7 8 9 3 6 3 5 4 4 3 5 2 *